Hi friends my name is Ashley, don't think that parents do so much for us? It may be things you see and things you don't see. Good parents may not always get the credit that they deserve so let us learn a few things that we as kids can do to begin to show appreciation for what our parents do for us every day such as

...

Like cleaning the kitchen such as washing or drying dishes, sweeping and or moping the floor wiping down the cabinet, counter, and table

Cleaning the living room such as removing things from the couch, wiping down the tv and tables, and sweeping and mopping the floor

Cleaning the bathroom such as wiping down the mirror cleaning the sink, tub, toilet, sweeping and or mopping the floor

Brushing your teeth, washing your face, and taking a bath.

Make sure you eat all of your fruits
and veggies

Getting dressed on
your own

Do all of your homework and ask for help when you need it.

Cleaning your room by straightening your bed, picking up your toys, sweeping, or mopping the floor.

I love helping my parents, how about you? Now what can you do to help your parents?

Other books by this author available on Amazon

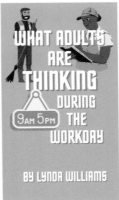

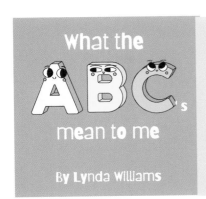

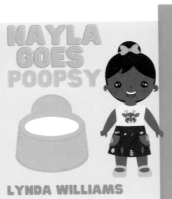

Printed in Great Britain
by Amazon

24422647R00016